AQUAPONICS
The Best ways to Grow Aquaponic Plants

© Copyright 2016

All rights Reserved. No part of this book may be reproduced in any form without permission in writing from the author. Reviewers may quote brief passages in reviews.

Disclaimer

No part of this publication may be reproduced or transmitted in any form or by any means, mechanical or electronic, including photocopying or recording, or by any information storage and retrieval system, or transmitted by email without permission in writing from the publisher.

While all attempts have been made to verify the information provided in this publication, neither the author nor the publisher assumes any responsibility for errors, omissions or contrary interpretations of the subject matter herein.

This book is for entertainment purposes only. The views expressed are those of the author alone, and should not be taken as expert instruction or commands. The reader is responsible for his or her own actions.

Adherence to all applicable laws and regulations, including international, federal, state and local laws governing professional licensing, business practices, advertising and all other aspects of doing business in the US, Canada, UK or any other jurisdiction is the sole responsibility of the purchaser or reader.

Neither the author nor the publisher assumes any responsibility or liability whatsoever on the behalf of the purchaser or reader of these materials. Any perceived slight of any individual or organization is purely unintentional.

Table of Contents

INTRODUCTION 1

CHAPTER 1 – CREATIVE GROWING WITH AQUAPONICS 3
- SPACE 3
- LIGHT 4
- WATER/NUTRIENTS 5
- HEAT 6

CHAPTER 2 – THE BASIC SYSTEM 7
- THE BUCKET 7
- THE FISH TANK 8
- THE MINI SYSTEM 9
- WHAT PLANTS? 11

CHAPTER 3 – GROW BEDS 13
- SIMPLE GROW BED 13
- BED CONSTRUCTION 15
- WHAT PLANTS? 17

CHAPTER 4 – VERTICAL GROWING 19
- STRAWBERRY TOWERS 19
- ZIPGROW TOWERS 21
- WHAT PLANTS? 22

CHAPTER 5 – GUTTERING 24
- FREESTANDING Z GUTTERING WALL 24
- WALL MOUNTED GUTTERS 26

    WHAT PLANTS? 27
CHAPTER 6 – INDOOR VS. OUTDOOR GROWING 28
    INDOOR 28
    OUTDOOR 29
    WHAT PLANTS? 31
CONCLUSION 32

Introduction

Aquaponics is a great way to grow fish and food together, but the biggest question for most people is how to grow. Since so many plants do well with aquaponics, it's easy to get over enthused and try and grow everything! With the right set up you can do this but it's also going to be much harder to have healthy plants if you're a beginner so it's a good idea to start out small. Similarly, even if you've picked out plants already growing them in a system that fits your space can be the bigger challenge.

An aquaponic system can be as small as a bucket with fish and a pot fitted on the top, but this is far from efficient. If you're comfortable with the basics of aquaponics, then this is the ideal guide for figuring out the best way to maximize your space and grow all the plants you want to.

The key to having a good aquaponic set up is making sure that your plants get their three main needs met – light, water, and nutrients. Since your water and nutrients are the same thing this means that the grow area has to be adequately saturated or your plants will fail to flourish; too much water, on the other hand, and they may rot. Without having the basics of aquaponic growing down you're already way ahead of yourself. This is meant as an intermediate guide for those already familiar with the basics of how aquaponics works.

When looking for starter plants you'll either want to source those already grown in a hydroponic environment or start them yourself from seeds.

Seed starting in aquaponics really isn't difficult. It's a good idea to start them in a material like coir or rock wool because these are small and will break apart to allow the root system to expand while still providing the support the growing root system needs. It's not advised to transplant plants from a soil environment because there's a huge risk of transplant shock. Similarly, transplanting plants from soil also means you can bring in bacteria and contaminants that may affect your fish. An aquaponic system is a delicate balance which needs to be maintained, both for the health of fish and plants.

To grow your plants well you sometimes have to get a little creative. It's not necessarily about having better equipment but about being smarter with what you have or can get!

What we're going to do is look at a few creative ways to grow your plants and tackle the common problems that plague many growers so that your plants will be the best they can!

Chapter 1 – Creative Growing with Aquaponics

If you're looking to find new ways of growing with aquaponics, then you're probably faced with a problem. While this type of gardening has its own challenges, sometimes we are faced with ones we just can't avoid. The biggest problem that most aquaponics enthusiasts face is space. You'll need enough space to deal with the tank, the grow beds (if you're using them), equipment, storage, access to water and power, and enough light for plants to grow. It's not an easy balance to achieve in the first place but when faced with an environment that isn't conducive to growing plants successfully sometimes you have to get creative.

Space

If your first obstacle is space, then you're going to need to look at growing upwards. This means creating vertical towers or guttering arrangements that are held above your fish tank. Your fish won't be affected by lower light, and it will help you keep the algae bloom down by shading the tank. Your compromise with such a system is that you're going to be limited on the type of plants you can grow. Plants that have large root systems or that require extra stabilization will not work in smaller containers. While this might seem like common sense, you can also look at different varieties as a way around the problem. For example, if you want to grow tomato plants but just can't give up the space for a large grow bed, compromise with a hanging variety that can be grown in guttering instead.

You can also maximize your space by growing your plants strategically. Grow large plants at the back or center of the grow box and grow smaller plants between the others or in front. This will give you the option of growing more plants per box than trying to grow all the same crops at the same time in each. As long as your system is flooding high enough to saturate the grow bed enough to reach all the plants, your only limit is how they are organized and whether you have enough fish to support them.

Light

If you're growing inside or trying to fit a lot of plants together, then lighting can be a problem. To get around this, consider using reflective panels indoors to maximize your light. Reflectors work to bounce any light rays that aren't aimed at your plants back at them. They also reflect heat, so if you're working with a system that needs heating (for example, in winter), then you won't be paying as much for heating by using reflectors. Reflectors can work outside, but because the sun's rays are so strong, they are not advised. A strong reflection can burn plants, melt plastic, and set fire to items, all of which can happen with sun rays when compared to weaker artificial light.

WATER/NUTRIENTS

There really isn't a compromise when it comes to the size of your pump. If there's one thing you should opt to go bigger with, it is the pump. The pump is what pushes water and nutrients around your system, and if it's not strong enough you'll find that the plants that are further from the water input may not get watered at all, or in a grow bed environment the water level may not reach the roots. Plants must have water and nutrients, or they will die, there is no compromise. What you can get creative with here is to have two smaller pumps as your system grows and create two smaller systems cycling off a large fish tank. This will also be a cost effective way of growing your system without wasting the pump equipment you already have.

Because your fish provide the nutrition, you also can't compromise on the size of your tank. Without enough fish, plants will not get the nutrients they need to thrive. Too many fish, and the overcrowding can cause disease, death, and fights depending on your variety. You can, however, compromise on your type of fish. Some fish are much larger than others and simply opting for a smaller variety can mean you'll be able to get more fish per tank. This will up your nutrient level in the water. The same can be said for choosing certain varieties of fish over others since they produce greater amounts of waste.

Heat

While most plants will not need extra heating in an indoor environment if you want to grow year-round you'll have to consider heating. Tropical fish species like Tilapia also require heating if you plan on growing year round in a non-tropical climate. To maximize your heat, insulate the fish tank well and consider adding a reflective cover in summer and a black one in winter if you're growing outside. Black absorbs heat while the reflective surface will direct it away on hot days. You can also help maximize your heat by using reflective panels on your lighting if you're indoors. The problem with this is that it's easy to overheat your plants and your fish so you'll also need a ventilation system.

So, the first thing to do when figuring out the best way to grow is to look at what problems you're facing with your space and tackle them accordingly. Let's see a few of the alternative ways you can set up a system to grow plants well.

Chapter 2 – The Basic System

Probably the most basic system is one that fits onto your desktop or windowsill. These small systems are designed to give you a taste of aquaponics without investing a lot of money or time. You generally don't have to monitor these as closely as a full sized system, but you're also going to be limited in the number of plants you can actually grow. Most desktop systems use goldfish or other small ornamental fish rather than edible fish, since you don't want the fish to outgrow the tank. While this means you're losing out on a food crop, it's also meant more as a learning experiment than actual farming. This is also the ideal way for children to learn about aquaponics. You'll want to add Organic Vitamin C rather than chemical water treatments to deal with the chloramines in tap water, since these are safe for plants.

The Bucket

The simplest aquaponic system is a five-gallon bucket. You can grow any small plant such as herbs or lettuce in this. Stick with only one or two plants at most. Place your plant into a basket filled with grow media. This can be coir, LECA, rockwool, etc. Make sure that the root system reaches the bottom of the basket so that the plant will have access to the water. There are two ways of supplying water and nutrients to this system. You can either place three goldfish into the bucket (approximately), or you can use the water from an already set up fish tank and drain it off to fill the bucket. You want the water level to reach the roots of the plant while the basket is suspended from the top. Ideally, your basket will fit comfortably into the top of the bucket and then the roots dangle into the water.

That's it! You've set up the most basic way to grow aquaponic plants.

The Fish Tank

This is a better system if you want to actually keep fish in it. The bucket isn't ideal because it's much harder to monitor your fish since you can't see them. It's also much more fun for children since they can watch the fish. For the fish tank system, you need a minimum 10-gallon fish tank. A goldfish bowl is really too small to work, since you will be constantly adding water and a single fish can't provide enough waste for a plant to survive.

You can use the same concept by filling the plant baskets with growing material, but it's advised not to use rockwool or coir with small fish. The reason for this is because the small particles of rockwool can get swallowed by the fish and cause them harm. Coir also rots and degrades which can change the balance of nutrients in the tank. Whatever the grow medium, make sure that it is well washed before using it in the tank.

This system and the bucket both use a method known as Deep Water Culture to work. This involves the plants being directly in contact with the water. These are the simplest and cheapest systems.

The Mini System

Similar to the fish tank, you can actually create a proper aquaponics system with a floodable grow bed that will fit in a corner. Because this system is more efficient, you can actually work with a much smaller tank. This can be done with a 5-gallon "critter" tank and as few as two fish. It is, however, more difficult to set up because you have to include a pump and tanks. The biggest problem people have with this system is that they do not flood the grow bed high enough to keep the roots saturated for even growth. A simple overflow system works well for this if you're working with less than six plants and a grow box no larger than 12x12". This is actually an ideal system to set up as a seed starter before transferring to a larger system as grown plants. You can use rockwool or coir for seed starters with this system with a filter.

Start by drilling a hole into the lid of the critter tank that is large enough to run clear plastic tubing through. This will run your water through the pump and into your grow bed so you won't need anything larger than an inch in diameter maximum. A small 10gph pump is more than adequate for this type of system, and you shouldn't need a heater unless you choose to get warm water fish. Line your tank with a little gravel, this helps the bacteria to develop. In your grow bed, cut a hole large enough to fit a simple strainer through (approx 2" diameter), seat the strainer and fill with a sponge. This will help catch solids that pass through your system and will stop them clogging up your pump. On top of the filter fill your grow bed about halfway up with media. This could be Hydroton, LECA or Perlite.

You can buy a simple side table or build a frame so that the grow bed sits directly above the fish tank. You'll want the filter to drain into the hole in the top, so the water returns to the fish from the grow bed. If you buy a side table, cut a hole in the top for the filter to fit through.

Place your plants directly into the grow bed with the tubing running from the pump into the grow bed. You'll need a very strong light source if you're keeping the system indoors. Most plants need a minimum of 50 watts for successful growth. This will also help to prevent mold. Since strong light promotes algae growth, it's a good idea to make one of your fish a Plecostomas, or algae eater.

If you find that your system isn't flooding enough for your plants to get adequate water, add your filter to an overflow siphon. Remove your plants and media from the grow bed then, using aquarium sealant, add a pipe that fits approximately 1" above the hole and 1" below. You can then sit the strainer filter into the top of the pipe. This will allow the water to flood up to the inch mark then overflow into the filter and back into the tank. You'll need to leave approximately 48 hours to make the sealant waterproof before returning it to your system.

With all three of these desktop systems you'll need to provide your fish with fish food. Use smaller feedings so that there isn't an excess of rotting food in the tank which can affect your nitrogen levels. Every few days you'll also need to add a little bit of water to keep the levels up and once a month change out 10% of the water to help prevent ammonia levels from rising too high.

What Plants?

With a small, limited system most plants don't work well. You need plants that don't require a lot of water or nutrition so that your system will work. Herbs like basil, chives, oregano, and mint are all great choices for a small system like this. You'll also have fresh grown herbs immediately available. If you're starting the herbs from seed use coir or rockwool plugs, since the seeds are very small.

You can also grow other plants like spinach or lettuce. Be aware that some plants will take up more space than others and will have a more elaborate root system. Lettuce is an easy beginner plant to grow but it requires deeper roots and more liquids to thrive, certain varieties will also grow big so you may only be able to fit one or two in a desktop system if you plan on growing them to maturity.

Avoid plants that are extremely tall or that have a large root system like tomatoes. You won't have enough fish or enough height to make this work for larger plants, especially if you're using DWC instead of the mini system as the weight alone will push the plant into the water.

Chapter 3 – Grow Beds

Grow beds are by far the most common way to grow aquaponic plants. The reason for this is that they are simple, effective, and you have a lot more flexibility with them. Essentially, you're scaling up the mini system with a larger fish tank, larger pump, and larger grow bed. You may also want to add in a heater with a larger tank to prevent rot and mold, especially if you want to keep your system outside. Grow beds perform four functions in your aquaponic arrangement—they provide filtration, plant hydration, plant nutrition, and a place for aeration.

When filling your grow bed, you'll need to choose a suitable media to fill it with. Your media needs to be something that can be sanitized, so it doesn't contaminate your tank, affect the pH, or poison the fish. It also needs to be porous enough to hold water and keep the roots hydrated. Plant roots need to grow in a stable media to be able to support the plant properly, but they also need enough access to air to provide the elements the plant needs. Plants get their nutrition through the roots, so the media is very important.

Simple Grow Bed

The simplest grow bed is a waterproof box that is about double the depth of your smallest plant's root system. There should be an entry pipe with water from your fish tank and a filtered exit to return the water to the fish tank or cycle it through another grow bed. With a grow bed you have two options for your plants. You can plant established plants directly into the grow bed, but this forces you to maintain the same arrangement and can make things difficult if you need to remove some plants but not disturb others. The more prudent choice is to grow your plants in grow baskets placed into your media.

A media-based system can have a variety of different ways for the nutrient water to flow through. Most are flood based which is what makes perlite an ineffective media. You'll want something that can't pass through your filter, that holds water, and that will not float. Hydroton, LECA, or even sand will work well. These all hold water which will stop your plant's roots from drying out between floodings, but will keep the plants stable. Sand is the heaviest choice and should only be used if you have a very sturdy system.

Bed Construction

For a small, simple grow bed, you can actually just use household totes from any store. These totes are lightweight, cheap, and easy to work with for drilling holes and adding tubes. If you want, you can also build more attractive or sturdier wooden boxes to go on the outside to camouflage them. The grow bed box needs to be non-porous, nontoxic, and big enough for your plants to thrive. It does not, however, need to be tall! The average grow bed is a mere 4" deep, but depending on what you want to grow you may go up to 12". One of the most confused items is that grow beds need to be 12" minimal depth. While it's important to research your plants first before building a grow bed that is too deep or too shallow, for most smaller plants 12" will leave you with a lot of extra, unnecessary height.

For more commercial sized beds growers often build a wooden structure and then line it with aquarium or pond plastic. This makes the wood waterproof and keeps costs reasonable while still allowing you to build a large grow bed. Many commercial growers also use the large, food grade plastic IBC drums from companies like ULINE since these come in a variety of sizes and are very suitable.

One of the most interesting "alternative" grow beds is a 60-gallon drum that has been cut in half vertically. These drums often have spouts at one end which are already designed for water to flow out of. If you decide to use drums, buy new, food grade ones as others may previously have been used for chemicals or pesticides and may have residue that can damage plants or fish. For a larger grow bed you can also use a cut rain barrel, these will actual provide an even deeper bed and work well for plants that have deep root systems or need extra stability. Be careful with the larger barrel that your roots can still reach the water level since the curved surface will force water down into the bottom of the bed.

If you are building a large grow bed, make sure you have a large enough pump to cycle it. Not having a pump that can cope with the size of bed means your plants will not get enough water or nutrients, and this is a common mistake when people "go big". In a small system, you can work with a pump as small as 10HP while a larger system with multiple beds needs at least one, if not more, 100HP pump.

As a beginner, your grow bed should be of a size that is an approximate 1:1 ratio with your fish tank, this will provide enough nutrients for your plants and enough filtration. You can actually grow successfully at ratios of up to 2:1 if you're experienced. If you want to make things very simple, there are plenty of stores that sell ready set up "grow beds" which you can use. These are all the industry standard 30cm as this is what the majority of people still stick to.

What Plants?

As you can make your grow bed as deep as you need the grow bed system is suitable for all aquaponics plants. It is the only system that will work for taller or heavier plants like tomatoes, though. Larger plants require deep root systems and strong grow media to help support them. Tomatoes, peppers, roses, and other bush plants are all examples of plants that must be grown in a grow bed environment. Cucumbers, squash, and cabbage are also great for beds, but all these require a well-stocked fish tank since their nutritional needs are higher.

Carrots, beets, radishes, taro, and celeriac all work with aquaponics grow beds, the problem is that people struggle with potatoes and sweet potatoes. The answer to this is to use grow bags or to use a wicking type system of baskets. Most root crops need the pressure of soil to flourish which is why they fail in aquaponic environments. The top of the plants looks healthy, but the tuber crop is poor.

For the more adventurous grower, you can also grow trees in a grow bed! Seasoned growers will talk to you of success growing bananas, limes, oranges, pomegranate and even papaya!

The grow bed is the most versatile ways of growing aquaponically, but it's limited by the need for space. Grow beds need space, or the roots won't get properly aerated, plants will start to crowd, and they may not get enough nutrition. This means that if you're only working with a limited area, you may be limited to one grow bed directly above the fish tank. If you don't want to be forced into this arrangement, then you'll have to look elsewhere for space.

Chapter 4 – Vertical Growing

It's often said that people don't look any further than the end of their nose when trying to find a solution. Grow beds are such an obvious choice for aquaponics that many people simply bemoan not having the space before realizing that the space they have is underutilized. No matter how small your area you have vertical options for growing your plants. These can include making the entire system vertical or simply growing with additional levels above your original grow bed. Vertical aquaponics have massive space advantage over traditional grow beds, but they also mean you're spending less time bending over, and you can simply swap out tubes once you're done with each crop rather than dismantling the whole system.

Strawberry Towers

One of the most common vertical additions in aquaponics is the strawberry tower. Strawberries are hardy, and they also trail well which means you're not so limited by the space of the hole they grow out of. Towers are an ideal addition to small systems because they can be hung or mounted on the wall. To build a strawberry tower or add it to an existing system all you need is a pump that is strong enough to support them and the standard aquaponic setup. Your pump keeps the water circulating so if you haven't got enough head coming out, the plants further away will likely not get fluids or nutrition.

Start by buying standard white PVC plumbing pipe from any hardware store that is a minimum of 3" in diameter. Cut the pipe to the desired length and then drill holes for the pipe to be bolted up or attached to the water inflow. You can also suspend the pipes with hooks on a racking system. Remember that if you're hanging the pipes they will be much heavier once filled with media, water, and plants.

Remember that if you are suspending your pipes you'll have 360-degree growth space. At each point where you wish to place a grow hole cut a line as wide as you need using a hacksaw. Drill 1/2" holes in the matching end caps for your pipes. This is where the water will return to the system. Secure the end cap with screws and aquarium sealant and then cure for 48 hours.

You'll need to be quick with this next part as the plastic can scorch easily. Using a heat torch and a wooden broom handle, heat the bottom of the cuts and a little to the outside to soften the plastic. Using a knife begin to pry the cut outwards and open, finish using the broom handle to make a spout large enough for your plants. Immediately place a cold, wet towel over the plastic to cool and set it.

Attach smaller pipes into the holes in the bottom caps and seal them. These only need to be long enough to fit into the main drainage pipe underneath, you can also use tubing. You can also place the same cap system on the top of the towers but it's not necessary, and you won't be able to use sealant since you'll need to be able to access the grow media for cleaning. Bolt the pipes into the wall or however you want to suspend them. Make sure your bolts also have rubber grommets in the holes to prevent water from leaking out. Once the pipes are situated, fill them with grow media. Attach the drainage pipe on the bottom and connect it to the returning water system with a filter. Take the outgoing water from your pump and run it through tubing to the top of the towers. Split the input into tubes trailing to each individual tower.

Make sure you run your system through to check for any leaks and if you're starting fresh allow it to stabilize before adding in plants.

Zipgrow Towers

While the DIY approach might appeal to many you can also skip making your towers and simply buy them. Zipgrow Towers are one of the most common types, and you can get them in 3ft and 5ft versions. You can also buy them in bulk loads of 50 if you plan on growing a large amount. The best part about the Zipgrow system is that it's modular based, you can add on towers or take away as necessary. The towers also come with media already installed, designed specifically to produce a better surface for aquaponic growing. The media is made of a fibrous material that can be sanitized and reused over again; it's designed to keep root temperatures stable and make transporting plants easier. The kits also come with wicking strips and hooks for hanging the towers.

The design of the towers is quite clever. The media is contained in a long, thin bag that fits into the tower. Plants are placed into the media bag and then "zipped" into the tower unit. The towers are very light weight, even with media in, which makes them easy to move or swap out. The towers are also guaranteed for 20 years. The company actually produces the entire aquaponic system for your plants to grow with including rafts, grow beds, and sprinkler systems to provide a drip system for water.

In fact, if you're still new to aquaponics you can also purchase their beginner bundle or their full bundle as well as a MyAqua Farm, which is an already set up aquaponics system – just add water, plants, and fish!

What Plants?

Because the vertical systems are not designed for tall or heavy plants, you need small and light items or trailing plants. Strawberries, beans, lettuce, or herbs work well. Trailing tomatoes can work but will require a lot of nutrients to flourish. Remember that you are going to be limited by your pipe diameter and the hole that your plant can fit in. You can also use these for ornamental plants or for edible flowers.

Chapter 5 – Guttering

While vertical towers are a great way to maximize your space vertically they are limited by how small the grow holes are. To compromise with this, you can use guttering instead. A guttering rack takes up the same space as a vertical line of towers; only it's built horizontally. Gutters stack on top of each other in a rack formation, just like the towers. The key with guttering though is that you have to be very careful not to lose light on the lower gutters. You can actually make this work with grow beds instead of gutters too as long as you attach lighting to the underside of the grow beds so that the upper levels aren't restricting plant growth.

Freestanding Z Guttering Wall

Unlike PVC pipes, gutters are much heavier. They allow you more space and can accommodate larger plants but also require more media. If you're growing with guttering, it's important to pick the lightest grow media your system will work with. Perlite is perfect if you are using a constant flood or NFT system since it is exceptionally light. Rockwool or LECA are also good alternatives depending on your plant choices.

The key with free standing guttering is using a Z-shape flow for the water, so that your water continues to push itself through without needing extra pump power, you can also use a drip arrangement where the gutters drip into each other from rather than pushing the water through if you want to save money, but this isn't as effective.

The real benefit of the Z system though is that you can actually make this work on a very small scale. The simplest system actually creates a very beautiful design which can trickle water back into the fish tank like a fountain. Your growing garden can then become a feature rather than just a convenient way to grow.

To start with, you'll need four large gutters with end caps for both ends. Cap and seal the gutters and then set aside. The easiest way to mount freestanding gutters is on an asymmetrical A-frame. Using lumber, construct two A-frames and connect them with a Z pattern of wood which your guttering will follow. For a less complicated version, you can also make each side of the frame different where the horizontal bars are and rest the guttering on these instead. Remember that you want one alternating side of each rail higher so that the water will flow. You want your gutters to be about 8" in height apart from top to bottom.

Bolt the gutters to the A-frames so that they're steady. Use grommets to prevent leaks and seal with aquarium sealant. Drill one 1/2" diameter hole at the end of each end cap or in the bottom of the gutter. Insert tubing into the hole and seal with sealant to plug, trail the other end into the bottom of the gutter below. From the lowest point of the bottom gutter, attach tubing to reach the filter and return the water back into your system.

Fill the gutters with light media and connect to your system. Cycle through to check for leaks.

Wall Mounted Gutters

To set up a guttering wall, you'll need similar methods to those of the strawberry towers. Deep rain guttering is available from most hardware stores and works perfectly for long, thin gutters. Alternatively, you can use common gutter planters from the garden center and seal up the drainage holes in the bottom. This will give you a deeper, wider gutter than house guttering and it's also sturdier if you plan on using larger plants.

You can run this over the top of your other tanks or create a bookshelf-type arrangement where they stack vertically to drain.

Instead of building the rack, start by lining out and creating supports on the wall for your gutters to bolt to. You'll want the same Z style arrangement that the rack uses where one side is higher than the other in an alternating pattern. Bolt your gutters to these supports and connect them using tubing like with freestanding rack. With the wall mounted gutters, you can also simply place them above the tank and have the bottom gutter drain through a filter directly over the fish tank which will save space and additional HP on the pump.

WHAT PLANTS?

When using guttering, you want to be careful not to use plants which will grow too high or which are too heavy for the system. Since your entire set-up is essentially balanced on bolts, this is best for herbs, ornamental plants, strawberries, greens, or trailing tomatoes. You'll want to avoid plants that grow tall like peppers, or anything bushy like roses.

As the Z Guttering is quite aesthetic, you can also use this method to grow ornamental plants and grasses quite successfully. Many people use a smaller version of this system to make a pretty garden water feature to practice aquaponics with before moving on to a larger food crop system.

Chapter 6 – Indoor vs. Outdoor Growing

Regardless of your design, aquaponics will work on both an indoor and outdoor scale. This is why it is so popular with commercial and household growers since it will fit into any underutilized space. There are benefits to both indoor and outdoor growing with aquaponics and also downsides. Before designing your system take a moment to think about where the best place to grow your crops will be. Plants need several things to grow successfully – light, air, nutrients, water, and warmth. Without any of these plants may grow, but will not thrive. Your water and nutrients will be taken care of by your fish, but everything else must be provided by you or the location.

Indoor

Indoor plants can grow anywhere. Your basement, the windowsill in the kitchen, even a small tank in the living room is big enough for a basic system. As with any system, you're limited by how much you want to invest and your space. A larger indoor system uses a lot of electricity because of the need for light. Plants need far more light than most people realize and this can often be a costly input. Commercial lights also put off a lot of heat, which may be beneficial for the plants but can also pose a fire hazard.

Growing indoors also negates the need for a heater in winter. Many people choose fish without thinking about their natural climates. Tilapia, for example, do not do well in cold water which means growers must buy heaters for them. The same is true of plants, during cold weather plants will not thrive and to grow year-round you have to have heating if you're outside. Because of this, indoor growing can end up being much cheaper.

It's also cheaper because you're going to have much less exposure to pests. Even in the most sanitized environment your plants will still get the occasional pest, but unlike outside, there's a lot less chance of that if they are indoors. While pests can be controlled to some degree outside it also requires additional costs to do so.

Another benefit to indoor growing is not being hampered by the seasons. Since you're able to climate control year round you can grow a variety of different foods year round. This includes produce that would otherwise be unavailable.

OUTDOOR

The main advantage to outdoor growing is that you have plentiful natural light. Many plants need upwards of 18 hours a day of lighting, and this can be very expensive if you have a large indoor system. Not only that, but excessive lighting means a large amount of heat and fireproofing for such a system as well as ventilation can be prohibitively expensive. If you're planning on an indoor system, it's often best to go small or at least very simple like the basic grow bed or desktop arrangement.

Another good reason to grow outside is that you won't need to worry about waterproofing your electrical system or about running cables through the house to work with electrical needs. You also won't have to worry about accidental flooding or leaks ruining floorboards or the interior of the house.

Outdoor systems are much simpler than indoor systems just because you don't have to run them year round. Many growers choose to take the cold months off to reset their systems, which can be a cost-effective choice.

What Plants?

When it comes to navigating indoor vs. outdoor, there's no compromise for good information on your plant types. Most plant types will have some form of key or code on their packaging to determine what "zone" they are suited for. While growing indoors will give you control over the environment you can still figure out if these zones are all compatible. Some plants like hotter environments while others prefer milder temperatures. Growing plants that work well together is the ideal way to make sure that no matter whether you're growing indoor or outdoor, everything will thrive.

Conclusion

Thank you again for reading this book!

I hope this book was able to help you to learn more about how to grow plants aquaponically and the best ways to do so. Not all plants are suitable for aquaponics but with a little creativity you can make even a small space work to produce plenty of healthy fish and plants together. Even if you're working with limited light, a tight garden, or just a windowsill, with some creative design work you can grow plants aquaponically.

The next step is to start looking at your space options and figuring out how you can grow horizontally and vertically. It's important not to forget that even if you have very little horizontal space, you can also grow upwards! You'll also need to take into account lighting and whether your pump is strong enough to add more grow beds or vertical options.

If you're struggling to figure out how to get your plants organized or get your system running right, start small and work from there. There's no requirement to have more than one crop, and there's no need to be stuck only using grow beds. Don't forget if you feel overwhelmed you can also order pre-made systems and towers which you can customize to fit your space.

Getting your plants to grow right means you're giving them ample opportunity and sometimes that means cutting down on the number of plants you want so that the ones you do have can thrive. Even if you have the space for vertical growing, be careful you don't block the light for the lower plants or remember to add lighting.

There are so many ways of growing aquaponic plants that anyone can do it. Hopefully, now you've got some new ideas and ways to accomplish this with your own system.

If you have enjoyed this book, please be sure to leave a review and a comment to let us know how we are doing so we can continue to bring you quality ebooks.

Thank you and good luck!

Check out another book by Sheila Brown

www.ingramcontent.com/pod-product-compliance
Lightning Source LLC
Chambersburg PA
CBHW070041230426
43661CB00005B/713